STUDY GUIDE

Discover ACTS
THE GENTILE CONNECTION

by
Neva Evenhouse

revised by
Carol Veldman Rudie

CRC Publications
Grand Rapids, Michigan

Unless otherwise noted, Scripture quotations in this publication are from the HOLY BIBLE, NEW INTERNATIONAL VERSION, © 1973, 1978, 1984, International Bible Society. Used by permission of Zondervan Bible Publishers.

Cover photo by SuperStock.

ISBN 1-56212-387-4

10 9 8 7 6 5 4 3 2 1

Contents

How to Study

The questions in this study booklet will help you discover for yourself what the Bible says. This is inductive Bible study—no one will tell you what the Bible says or what to believe. You will discover the message for yourself.

Questions are the key to inductive Bible study. Through questions you will search for the writers' thoughts and ideas. The prepared questions in this booklet are designed to help you in your quest for answers. You can and should ask your own questions too. The Bible comes alive with meaning for many people as they discover for themselves the exciting truths it contains. Our hope and prayer is that this booklet will help the Bible come alive for you.

Questions are designed to be used with the New International Version of the Bible, but other translations can also be used.

Step 1. Read the Bible passage several times. Allow the thoughts and ideas to sink in. Think about its meaning. Ask questions of your own about the passage.

Step 2. Answer the questions, drawing your answers from the passage. Remember that the purpose of the study is to discover what the Bible says. Write your answers in your own words. If you use Bible study aids such as commentaries or Bible handbooks, do so only after completing your own personal study.

Step 3. Apply the Bible's message to your own life and world. Ask yourself these questions: What is this passage saying to me? How does it challenge me? Comfort me? Encourage me? Is there a promise I should claim? A warning I should heed? For what can I give thanks? If you sense God speaking to you in some way, respond to him in a personal prayer.

Step 4. Share your thoughts with someone else if possible. This will be easiest if you are part of a Bible study group that meets regularly to share discoveries and discuss questions. If you would like to learn of a study group in your area or if you would like more information on how to start a small group Bible study, write to Discover Your Bible, 2850 Kalamazoo Ave. SE, Grand Rapids, MI 49560 or to P.O. Box 5070, STN LCD 1, Burlington, ON L7R 3Y8.

Introduction

The book of Acts is a sequel to the gospel of Luke, the third New Testament gospel. Acts chronicles the history of the early Christian church from the time of Christ's ascension into heaven to Paul's imprisonment in Rome, a span of about thirty years. Written around A.D. 60 by Paul's beloved friend and physician, Luke, its purpose is to give Theophilus (a Roman believer) an accurate historical record of Christianity. Luke was aware of distorted rumors about Christianity and was concerned about clearing the early Christians of charges of rebellion and subversion. On all counts he shows that the Jews' angry opposition was responsible for the disturbances in various cities and that the Roman authorities had repeatedly cleared the Christians of all charges. The book is historical in nature, accurately naming the Roman emperor, various governors, and other authorities. All historical references have been documented to show the authenticity of Luke's writings.

Although the book is called the Acts of the Apostles, a more accurate title might be the Acts of the Holy Spirit, because the Spirit empowered the apostles and directed them in spreading the gospel. Acts gives a thrilling account of the early church, the opposition it faced and overcame, and the problems with which it dealt. It tells how the Holy Spirit guided and enabled the apostles and ordinary believers to follow Christ's command to boldly preach the good news of salvation from Jerusalem to Judea, Samaria, and throughout the Gentile world. By means of their witness, "the word of God continued to increase and spread" (Acts 12:24).

Glossary of Terms

angel—messenger of God who carries out his will in this world and serves those who belong to God.

Antioch—the name of two cities, one in Greece and one in Syria.

apostle—means "one sent out." The disciples were given this title after Jesus returned to heaven. They were the leaders in the early Christian church and were to verify that the events and interpretation of Jesus' life were correctly communicated.

Areopagus—either the hill by that name in the city of Athens (also called Mars Hill) or more probably the Athenian Supreme Court, which met at that location. During the time of the Roman empire, this court had authority only over religious and moral matters.

Artemis—Greek goddess of fertility.

Asia—Roman province in western Asia Minor.

baptize—to immerse someone in or sprinkle with water. This act identifies a new believer with Christ and symbolizes the washing away of sin through Christ's sacrifice on the cross.

baptism of John—John the Baptist preached and also baptized with water those who confessed their sins as a sign that they had been spiritually cleansed. He began his work before Jesus started preaching and predicted that Jesus' ministry would be greater than his.

Barnabas—a native of Cyprus and one of the early converts in Jerusalem who shared his wealth with all the believers there.

Caesaria—its excellent harbor made it the natural gateway to Judea and the headquarters of the Roman government.

centurion—one of six to ten commanders in a typical Roman regiment. These men commanded at least one hundred men and were carefully selected for their leadership qualities.

Christian—one who belongs to Christ.

church—usually used in Acts to mean a local groups of believers. Mentioned in the Bible for the first time in Acts 5:11.

circumcision—the Jewish rite of cutting off the foreskin of the penis as a sign of belonging to God's people. It symbolized cutting away sin from one's life and living faithfully to God.

Claudius—emperor of Rome from A.D. 41-54.

clean—God allowed the Jews to eat certain kinds of animals and to use them for sacrifices. These were referred to as "clean." All other animals were considered "unclean." Mixing both types of animals together caused them all to be "unclean."

Corinth—great city and commercial center that was famous for its immorality.

Damascus—although located in the province of Syria, this important city had a large Jewish population and was the most important city close to Judea.

David—second Old Testament king of Israel and a direct ancestor of Jesus. He was a national hero among the Jews of Jesus' day. His story can be found in 1 Samuel 16-1 Kings 2:12.

death with the sword—beheading.

devil—either the leader of the spiritual beings opposed to God or one of the individual demons in that group.

disciple—one who follows a leader or teacher.

Ephesus—the capital of the province of Asia, situated at the junction of neutral trade routes and therefore a wealthy commercial city. It was home to the temple of the Greek goddess of fertility, Artemis, which was one of the seven wonders of the ancient world.

elders—leaders of the local Jewish community or synagogue. This form of governing also was evident in the early church.

Epicureans—one of two prominent schools of philosophy in Athens, which taught that pleasure was the highest good.

faith—abandoning all trust in one's own resources. Saving faith consists of the certain knowledge that what God has revealed in the Bible is true and a confidence that all one's sins are forgiven for Jesus' sake.

fasting—going without food in order to express repentance and sorrow for sin.

fear of the Lord—awe of God's power and holiness, combined with love for God and obedience to his will.

Feast of Unleavened Bread—a Jewish feast day that celebrated the Lord's deliverance of Israel from the bondage of slavery in Egypt.

Galilee—the Roman province in northern Palestine where Jesus grew up in the town of Nazareth.

Gentiles—people outside the Jewish faith and not of the Jewish race.

God-fearing—a term to describe a non-Jewish person who followed Jewish religious practices.

Grecian Jews—although religiously and ethnically Jewish, this group had become integrated into the Gentile world by speaking Greek and adopting some Greek opinions and practices.

hanging on a tree—crucifixion.

Hermes—the Greek god who is the herald or messenger of the other gods. His Roman name is Mercury.

Herod—Agrippa I, the grandson of Herod the Great who ruled when Jesus was born.

high priest—the spiritual and political leader of the Jews; the head of the Sanhedrin.

Holy Spirit—the third person of the Trinity. The Holy Spirit lives in the hearts of believers to guarantee that they will receive all of God's promises and to empower them to live holy lives.

James—one of Jesus' brothers.

John Mark—cousin of Barnabas.

John the Baptist—a cousin of Jesus. He had been set apart before birth to prepare the way for Jesus' coming.

Judea—a Roman province in southern Palestine that includes the cities of Bethlehem and Jerusalem.

justified—declared forgiven and righteous by God through repentance and faith in Jesus Christ. Those who are justified are not merely pardoned: the demands of the law have been fully met through the atoning work of Christ.

law—the Ten Commandments and hundreds of ceremonial and civil laws given by God to the nation of Israel and recorded in the Old Testament. The term also refers to a section of the Scriptures that was read in the synagogue.

Mary—an aunt of Barnabas.

memorial offering—the part of the grain offering that was burned at the altar during sacrifice to represent the rest of the grain given to the Lord.

Nazareth—a small town in the province of Galilee where Jesus grew up.

Passover—an annual, seven-day Jewish celebration commemorating God's deliverance of the Jews from slavery in Egypt. All Jewish men were required to celebrate Passover in Jerusalem, bringing their families from all over the Roman Empire.

Paul—Greek form of the Hebrew name Saul. Jewish people usually had both a Greek and a Hebrew name.

Pharisees—one of three main Jewish sects and the one with the strictest rules about the importance of observing the Old Testament laws. Pharisees also adhered to regulations that were not written in the law of Moses but were merely traditions passed down by their ancestors.

Philip—one of the seven men selected by the Jerusalem believers to assist in the distribution of supplies to the poor and widows of the church.

Philippi—Macedonian city founded as a Roman colony for retired soldiers. Few Jews settled there.

Pilate—Roman ruler of Judea who was forced by the Jewish leaders to condemn Jesus to death.

placing hands on—a gesture indicating blessing, the giving of authority, or the bestowing of the Holy Spirit.

proconsul—governor of a Roman province. Provinces were controlled by the Roman senate.

prophesy—often means to foretell the future but also, and more frequently, to speak the word of God.

Prophets—section of the Old Testament that was read in the Jewish synagogue.

prophets—wandering preachers dedicated to listening for the word of God and speaking it publicly.

Sabbath—the Jewish holy day, which fell on Saturday, and which was to be used for worship and rest.

saints—people who belong to God. In the New Testament, saints were people who were born again and lived by faith in Jesus Christ.

Samaria—the Roman province north of Jerusalem whose people were despised by the Jews because they were ethnically mixed, because they kept a version of the Jewish law not acceptable to the Jews, and because they worshiped in their own temple on Mount Gerizim.

Simon—Peter's Jewish name.

speaking in tongues—the ability, given by the Holy Spirit, to speak foreign languages without previous instruction.

Stoics—adherents of a prominent school of philosophy in Athens that taught self-sufficiency and the absence of emotion.

synagogue—the building in which local Jews gathered for religious instruction, worship, and prayer. The synagogue did not have one official minister. Instead, competent members of the congregation or visitors were invited to give the sermon. The Scriptures were read from a standing position as a sign of reverence, while the message was delivered in a sitting position at the front. Found throughout the empire, synagogues could be organized if ten Jewish men were present.

tanner—person who took raw animal skins and turned them into leather. According to Jewish law, a tanner would be ritually unclean because of his work with dead animals.

Tarsus—city in the Roman province of Asia where Paul grew up.

teachers—men in the local churches whose duty it was to instruct new Christians.

tearing one's clothes—done as a sign of great grief.

unclean—Jewish religious practice was regulated by various distinctions between things that were acceptable and things that were not. Contact with ritually "unclean" things made a person unfit for worship and required various elaborate rituals to remedy. The purpose of these distinctions, including the ones regarding food and contact with foreigners, was to preserve Israel's distinctiveness as God's people.

vision—special experience in which God personally reveals his will to a person chosen for special service.

the Way—used occasionally in Acts to refer to the Christian faith.

witness—a legal term describing those who could testify to an action. In the Old Testament, two or three witnesses were required in order to convict a person of a crime.

Zeus—the head of the Greek gods, later known by the Romans as Jupiter.

Mitylene
Miles 0 100 200 300
Kms 0 100 200 300 400 500
GALATIA
Smyrna
ASIA
Antioch
PISIDIA
Iconium
CAPPADOCIA
SAMOS
Ephesus
Colosse
Lystra
Derbe
Cilician Gates
PATMOS
PAMPHYLIA
CILICIA
Tarsus
Cos
Attalia
Perga
Cnidus
LYCIA
Rhodes
Patara
Antioch
Myra
Seleucia
RHODES
Mark—to Jerusalem
SYRIA
Orontes R.
Salamis
CYPRUS
Paphos

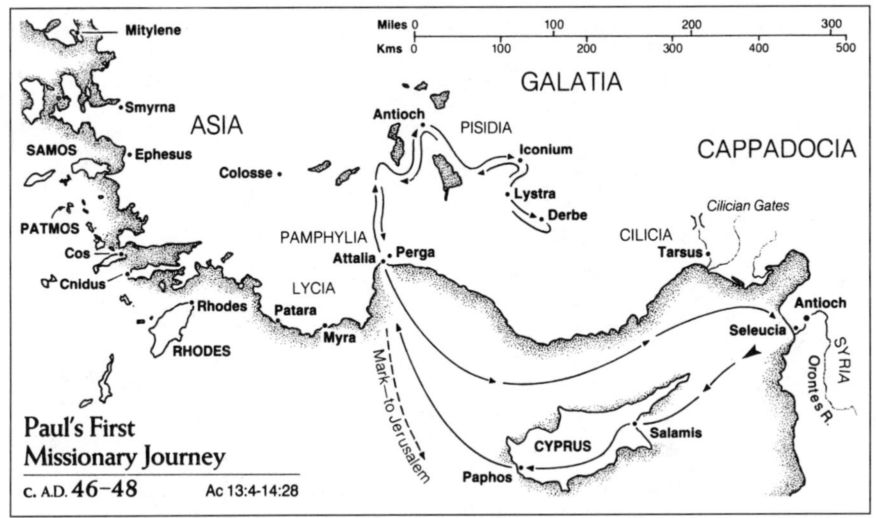

Paul's First Missionary Journey

c. A.D. 46–48 Ac 13:4-14:28

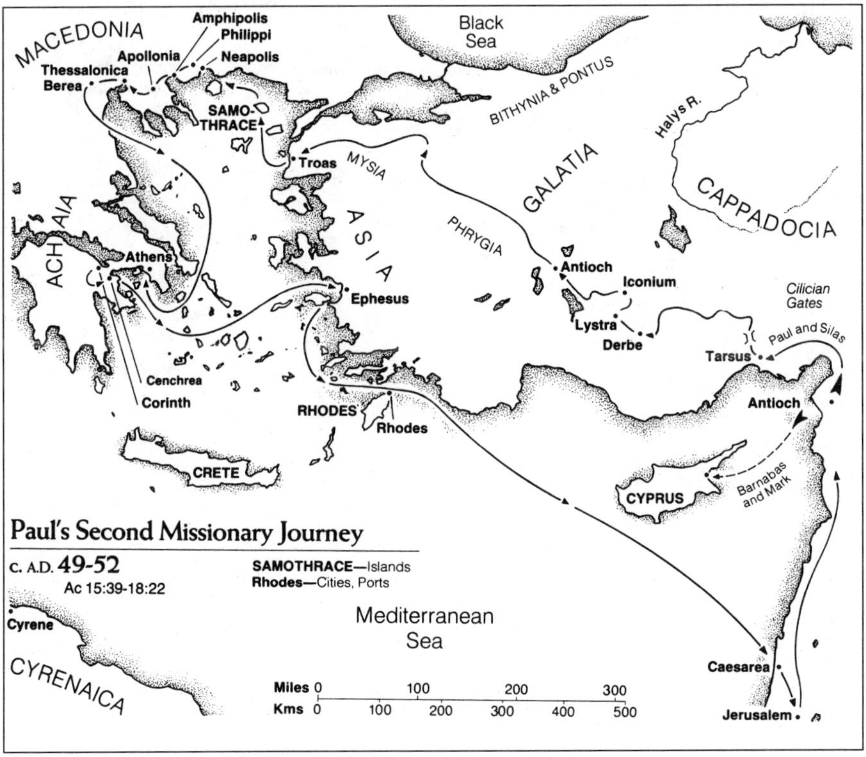

Amphipolis
MACEDONIA
Philippi
Black Sea
Apollonia
Neapolis
Thessalonica
Berea
BITHYNIA & PONTUS
SAMO-THRACE
Halys R.
Troas
MYSIA
GALATIA
CAPPADOCIA
ACHAIA
ASIA
PHRYGIA
Athens
Antioch
Iconium
Ephesus
Cilician Gates
Lystra
Derbe
Paul and Silas
Tarsus
Cenchrea
Corinth
Antioch
RHODES
Rhodes
CRETE
CYPRUS
Barnabas and Mark
Mediterranean Sea
Cyrene
CYRENAICA
Miles 0 100 200 300
Kms 0 100 200 300 400 500
Caesarea
Jerusalem

Paul's Second Missionary Journey

c. A.D. 49-52 Ac 15:39-18:22

SAMOTHRACE—Islands
Rhodes—Cities, Ports

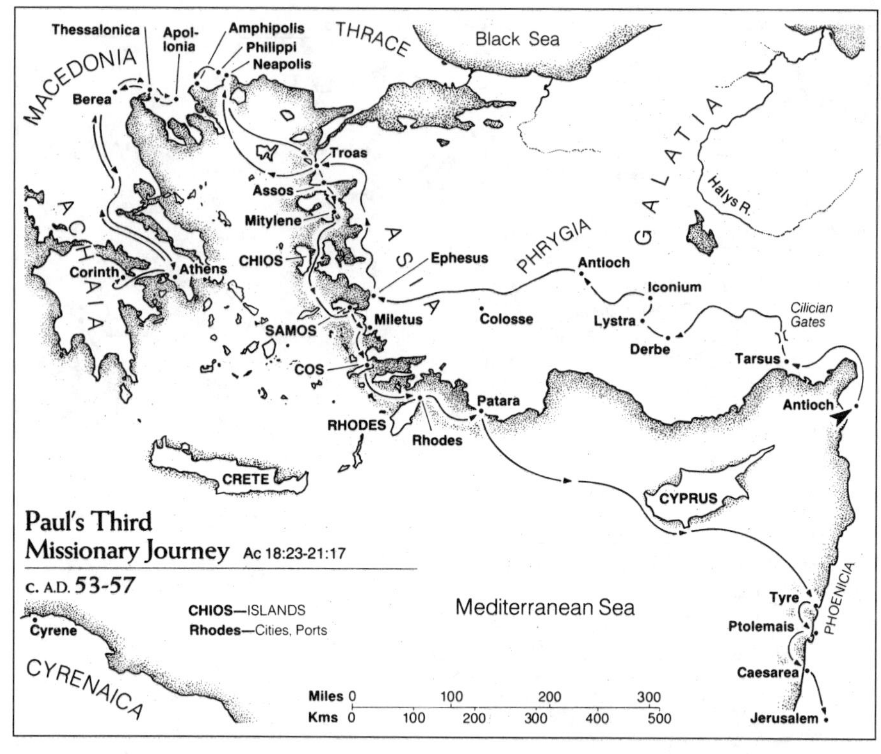
Thessalonica
Apol-
lonia
Amphipolis
Philippi
Neapolis
THRACE
Black Sea
MACEDONIA
Berea
Troas
Assos
Mitylene
CHIOS
Ephesus
ASIA
PHRYGIA
GALATIA
Halys R.
Antioch
Iconium
Lystra
Derbe
Cilician
Gates
Tarsus
Antioch
ACHAIA
Corinth
Athens
SAMOS
Miletus
Colosse
COS
RHODES
Rhodes
Patara
CRETE
CYPRUS
Paul's Third
Missionary Journey Ac 18:23-21:17
c. A.D. 53-57
CHIOS—ISLANDS
Rhodes—Cities, Ports
Mediterranean Sea
Tyre
Ptolemais
PHOENICIA
Caesarea
Jerusalem
Cyrene
CYRENAICA
Miles 0 100 200 300
Kms 0 100 200 300 400 500

Lesson 1

Acts 8:1-3; 9:1-31

Conversion and Calling

1. *Acts 8:1-3; 9:1-2*

   a. What was the situation of the church at this time?

   b. What do Saul's actions tell us about him?

2. *Acts 9:3-6*

   How is Saul's plan thwarted?

3. *Acts 9:7-9*

   What details of the story does Luke relate here? What might be significant about each one?

4. *Acts 9:10-19*

   a. What does the Lord reveal to Ananias about Saul?

   b. How does Ananias react to the Lord's commands?

   c. What happens to Saul as a result?

5. *Acts 9:20-25*

   a. How does Luke describe the new Saul?

   b. How do different groups react to Saul?

6. *Acts 9:26-30*

   a. How do the disciples in Jerusalem respond to Saul when he returns?

   b. What changes their attitude?

   c. What does Saul continue to do in Jerusalem?

7. *Acts 9:31*

   a. What enables the church to enjoy a time of peace?

   b. What effect does this peace have on the church?

8. *Acts 8:1-3; 9:1-31*

   a. What does Saul's experience tell us about the cost of following Jesus?

   b. How has God used events and people to help his church grow?

   c. How has the Holy Spirit worked in the lives of individual believers and in the church as a whole?

Lesson 2
Acts 9:32-10:23

Clean and Unclean

1. *Acts 9:32-35*
   a. What does Peter do in these verses?

   b. What is the result of the man's healing?

2. *Acts 9:36-38*
   a. What kind of person is Dorcas?

   b. Why do the disciples at Joppa call for Peter?

3. *Acts 9:39-43*
   a. How are the disciples in Joppa reacting to Dorcas's death?

   b. What does Peter do?

   c. What is the result of his actions?

4. *Acts 10:1-8*

   a. Who was Cornelius?

   b. Why and how does God respond to this man?

5. *Acts 10:9-16*

   a. What happens to Peter on the rooftop?

   b. How does Peter's sense of religious duty differ from the Lord's direction?

6. *Acts 10:17-23*

   a. What happens while Peter is pondering his vision?

   b. What is the connection between Peter's vision and the mission of Cornelius's servants?

7. *Acts 9:32-10:23*

   a. How does Peter's leadership help the church expand?

   b. In what ways does God build his church?

Lesson 3

Acts 10:23-11:18

No Favoritism

1. *Acts 10:23-26*
   a. How is Peter characterized in these verses?

   b. What do we learn about Cornelius? About his faith?

2. *Acts 10:27-29*
   a. Why has Peter come?

   b. What is his attitude toward the Gentiles?

3. *Acts 10:30-35*
   a. How would you summarize Cornelius's answer to Peter's question?

   b. What does Peter learn about Cornelius?

c. What does he learn about God?

d. How do you think he reaches these conclusions?

4. *Acts 10:36-43*

a. According to Peter, what do his listeners already know?

b. What more does he want them to know? For what reason?

5. *Acts 10:44-48*

a. On whom does the Holy Spirit come? Why?

b. How do Peter and his companions react to this event?

c. What have they learned about God's plan for his church?

6. *Acts 11:1-3*

   a. How do the Jerusalem believers react to this new Gentile group?

   b. What motivates their reaction?

7. *Acts 11:4-18*

   a. How does Peter respond to the situation?

   b. Why do you think he responds in this way?

   c. How would you summarize Peter's explanation? What added insight does he include that was not recorded earlier?

   d. How do the believers react to Peter's explanation?

8. *Acts 10:23-11:18 (also review Acts 10:1-22)*

   a. How has the Lord prepared Peter and the believers to know and do his will more fully?

   b. What might be the significance of this event today?

Lesson 4

Acts 11:19-12:25

The True King

1. *Acts 11:19-21*

   What has caused the church's growth in Antioch?

2. *Acts 11:22-26*

   a. Why did the church of Jerusalem send Barnabas to Antioch?

   b. What does he find in Antioch? How does he respond?

   c. What new name is given to the believers in Antioch?

3. *Acts 11:27-30*

   What do these verses tell us about the church at Antioch?

4. *Acts 12:1-5*

   a. What does Herod do? Why?

b. What happens to Peter?

c. How does the church respond to Peter's imprisonment?

5. *Acts 12:6-11*

a. What precise details does Luke include in this passage?

b. What does Peter conclude?

6. *Acts 12:12-17*

a. Where does Peter go?

b. What kinds of responses does he receive?

7. *Acts 12:18-25*

a. How do the guards react to Peter's escape? What does their reaction tell us?

b. How does Herod respond to the situation?

c. What do the people from Tyre and Sidon want? How do they go about getting it?

d. What happens to Herod? Why?

e. What contrasts between Herod and God are brought out in this passage?

8. *Acts 11:19-12:25*

a. In what ways do we see the early church growing in this lesson?

b. How does the Lord demonstrate his power on behalf of the church?

Lesson 5

Acts 13:1-43

Seeing and Believing

1. *Acts 13:1-5*
   a. What can we learn from these verses about the church at Antioch and about the people Luke mentions?
   b. What is the work for which Barnabas and Saul are set apart? How does this come about?
2. *Acts 13:6-12*
   a. Who is Elymas (Bar-Jesus)? What problem does he pose for Saul and Barnabas?
   b. What does Paul do about it? Why?
   c. What causes the proconsul to believe?

3. *Acts 13:13-15*

What can we learn from these verses about Barnabas, Paul, and John Mark? About their method of ministering?

4. *Acts 13:16-23*

What is Paul's main point in this part of his sermon?

5. *Acts 13:24-25*

   a. How does Paul view John the Baptist's work?

   b. Why might Paul be relating these facts?

6. *Acts 13:26-37*

   a. How had the Jewish leaders reacted to Jesus?

   b. What does Paul say about Jesus in these verses?

   c. How does he support what he says?

7. *Acts 13:38-41*

a. Whom is Paul addressing?

b. What is the "good news" Paul is bringing to his listeners?

c. How does Paul want his listeners to respond? Why?

d. What response does he not want? Why?

8. *Acts 13:42-43*

a. How do Paul's listeners react to his sermon?

b. How do Paul and Barnabas follow up this response?

9. *Acts 13:1-43*

a. What motivation do Paul and Barnabas have for preaching?

b. What methods do the two men develop in their work?

c. What is the central message of their preaching?

Lesson 6

Acts 13:44-14:28

The Door of Faith

1. ***Acts 13:44-45 (also review the previous lesson)***
   a. Why does nearly everyone in the city gather?

   b. How do the Jews react?

2. ***Acts 13:46-48***
   a. How do Paul and Barnabas interpret the Jews' reaction? What do they do in response?

   b. How do Paul's quotes from the Old Testament help make his point?

   c. How do the Gentiles respond?

3. ***Acts 13:49-52***
   a. What varied reactions does Luke record in this passage?

   b. What do you think caused these reactions?

4. *Acts 14:1-7*

   a. What do these verses say about Paul and Barnabas's work in Iconium?

   b. How does the outcome in Iconium compare with that in Pisidian Antioch (13:49-52)?

5. *Acts 14:8-13*

   a. What brings about the healing of the lame man at Lystra?

   b. What is the crowd's reaction?

6. *Acts 14:14-20*

   a. What message are the apostles trying to impress on the people at Lystra?

   b. How do Paul's approach and message here differ from his method in Pisidian Antioch (13:16-41)? Why do you think they differ?

   c. What happens to Paul as a result?

7. *Acts 14:21-28*

   a. What do these verses tell us about Paul and Barnabas's work?

   b. What is their primary reason for returning to each city?

   c. Why do Paul and Barnabas report back to the church at Antioch? (read also Acts 13:1-3)

8. *Acts 13:44-14:28*

   a. What teaching methods do Paul and Barnabas develop on this first missionary journey?

   b. How would you summarize their message?

   c. What was the reason for their success? For the opposition they encountered?

Lesson 7

Acts 15:1-35

Saved by Grace

1. *Acts 15:1-2 (review also Acts 11:20-26)*
   a. What controversy arises at the church in Antioch? How does it come about?

   b. What does the church do about it?

2. *Acts 15:3-4*
   a. What do Paul and Barnabas do as they travel to Jerusalem?

   b. What is the response to their news?

3. *Acts 15:5-6*

   What question do the apostles and elders address at their meeting?

4. *Acts 15:7-11*

   What is Peter's basic argument to the council?

5. *Acts 15:12*

   a. How do Paul and Barnabas support Peter?

   b. How does the assembly respond?

6. *Acts 15:13-21*

   a. What judgment does James make about the inclusion of the Gentiles?

   b. On what does he base his opinion?

   c. What solution does James recommend?

   d. What is his reason for this solution?

7. *Acts 15:22-35*

   a. What does the Jerusalem church decide to do?

   b. How does the church at Antioch respond?

   c. What is the result for the church as a whole?

8. *Acts 15:1-35*

   What is the significance of this episode for the early church?

Lesson 8

Acts 15:36-16:15

Another Continent

1. *Acts 15:36*

   a. What do Paul and Barnabas decide to do?

   b. What does their plan tell us about them?

2. *Acts 15:37-41*

   a. What is the cause of Paul and Barnabas's disagreement?

   b. What does this conflict reveal about both men?

   c. What results from this disagreement?

   d. What effect does Paul's ministry have?

3. *Acts 16:1-5*

   a. How does Luke portray Timothy?

   b. Why does Paul circumcise him?

   c. What is accomplished as a result of Paul's visits?

4. *Acts 16:6-10*

   a. How is Paul's itinerary determined (and not determined)?

   b. What is his mission?

5. *Acts 16:11-13*

   What does Luke reveal here about the progress and strategy of this missionary journey?

6. *Acts 16:14-15*

   a. Who is Lydia?

b. How does she respond to Paul's message?

7. ***Acts 15:36-16:15***

a. How is God's leading evident in the events recorded in these passages?

b. How does God's leading affect the church?

Lesson 9

Acts 16:16-17:15

Believe and Be Saved

1. *Acts 16:16-18*
   a. What situation do the missionaries encounter?

   b. Why is Paul upset? What does he do about it?

2. *Acts 16:19-24*
   a. What motivates those who opposed Paul and Silas?

   b. What is the accusation against them?

   c. How are Paul and Silas treated?

3. *Acts 16:25-30*
   a. What does this situation tell us about Paul and Silas's faith? About their character?

b. What do we learn about the other prisoners?

c. How does the jailer react to the situation?

4. *Acts 16:31-34*

a. What is Paul's response to the jailer's question?

b. What do these verses tell us about salvation?

c. How does the jailer react to the message?

5. *Acts 16:35-40*

a. How does Paul respond to the order for release? How is he treated as a result?

b. What do Paul and Silas do before they leave Philippi?

6. *Acts 17:1-9*

   a. How is Paul received by different groups in Thessalonica?

   b. Why do these groups react as they do?

7. *Acts 17:10-15*

   How is the response in Berea similar to that in Thessalonica? How is it different?

8. *Acts 16:16-17:15*

   What does this lesson tell us about Christianity's impact on the lives of individuals and communities?

Lesson 10

Acts 17:16-18:22

The Very Righteous

1. *Acts 17:16-21*

   a. How would you describe the city of Athens and its inhabitants?

   b. How does Paul respond to what he observes?

   c. How do people react to Paul's preaching?

2. *Acts 17:22-23*

   a. What do Paul's opening remarks tell us about him?

   b. How does Paul address his listeners?

3. *Acts 17:24-29*

   a. What does Paul say about the "unknown god" and its relationship to people?

b. According to Paul, how can people become aware of God?

c. How does God want people to respond to him?

d. What is the wrong way to respond? Why is it wrong?

4. ***Acts 17:30-34***

a. According to Paul, what does God now require of people?

b. On what basis does God make this requirement?

c. How do people respond to Paul?

5. ***Acts 18:1-4***

What does Paul do in Corinth?

6. ***Acts 18:5-8***

How does Paul's ministry in Corinth change? What causes these changes?

7. Acts 18:9-11

What assurances does the Lord give Paul?

8. Acts 18:12-17

a. Of what is Paul accused?

b. What is the outcome of his trial?

9. Acts 18:18-22

a. How does Paul conclude his missionary trip?

b. What established patterns does he follow?

10. Acts 17:16-18:22

a. In what ways has the gospel reached out to new groups of people?

b. How have both personal human initiative and the Lord's guidance been demonstrated in this journey?

c. How would you characterize the positive and negative effects of this journey?

Lesson 11

Acts 18:23-19:20

Baptism by the Spirit

1. *Acts 18:23*

   What was Paul's plan at the beginning of his third journey?

2. *Acts 18:24-28*

   a. How do these verses describe Apollos?

   b. What was lacking in his knowledge of the way of God? How did his fellow Christians remedy this?

   c. How does Apollos help the believers in Achaia (Greece)?

3. *Acts 19:1-7*

   a. What does Paul learn about the twelve Ephesian disciples after questioning them?

   b. What does Paul do for the disciples? What resulted?

4. *Acts 19:8-12*

   a. What methods does Paul use in Ephesus?

   b. What are the results of his work?

5. *Acts 19:13-17*

   a. What was wrong with the activities of the seven sons of Sceva?

   b. What ultimately results from this incident?

6. *Acts 19:18-20*

   a. What causes the public bonfire?

   b. How does this affect the spread of the gospel?

7. *Acts 18:23-19:20*

   a. In what specific ways has the Holy Spirit been evident in this visit to Ephesus?

   b. How has the message of salvation been advanced?

Lesson 12

Acts 19:21-20:12

The Church Defended and Encouraged

1. *Acts 19:21-22*

   What do these verses tell us about Paul's plans?

2. *Acts 19:23-27*

   a. What was the cause of the disturbance?

   b. What does this reaction tell us about Paul's ministry in Ephesus?

3. *Acts 19:28-34*

   a. What is the reaction of the silversmiths? Of other residents of Ephesus? Of Paul and his friends?

   b. What motivated these reactions?

4. *Acts 19:35-41*

   a. What argument does the city clerk use to quiet the crowd?

   b. What does the clerk's defense of Paul (v. 37) suggest about Paul's ministry to the Ephesians?

5. *Acts 20:1-6 (review also 19:21-22)*

a. What are Paul's reasons for moving on?

b. What characterizes this part of his journey?

6. *Acts 20:7-12*

a. What do these verses tell us about the church at Troas?

b. What do we learn about Paul in this episode?

c. What was the effect of this event on the church at Troas?

7. *Acts 19:21-20:12*

a. What characteristics of the early church are illustrated in this lesson?

b. What means does the Lord use to protect and advance the church?

c. How does the gospel affect the people in Ephesus as compared to those in Troas? What might account for the difference?

Lesson 13

Acts 20:13-21:16

On to Jerusalem

1. *Acts 20:13-17*

   What do we learn from these verses about Paul and his plans?

2. *Acts 20:18-21*

   a. How does Paul summarize his work in Asia?

   b. What things had Paul taught in Ephesus?

3. *Acts 20:22-24*

   a. How does Paul react to his knowledge of the future?

   b. Why does he react this way?

4. *Acts 20:25-31*

   a. Of what is Paul innocent? Why?

   b. What responsibilities does Paul give the elders?

   c. What dangers does Paul foresee for the church at Ephesus?

5. *Acts 20:32-38*

   a. What does Paul say about himself?

   b. Why does he say this to the Ephesian elders?

   c. How would you describe Paul's relationship to the Ephesian elders?

6. *Acts 21:1-9*

   How does Luke communicate a sense of foreboding in this journey?

7. *Acts 21:10-16*

a. What happens while Paul and his companions are at Philip's home?

b. How does Paul's reaction to Agabus's prophecy differ from that of his friends? What accounts for the difference?

8. *Acts 9:1-21:16*

a. How has the church grown through this section of Acts?

b. How has the Holy Spirit been involved in this growth?

c. How has the Spirit been reflected in the attitudes and actions of different individuals and groups?

Evaluation Questionnaire

DISCOVER ACTS—THE GENTILE CONNECTION

As you complete this study, please fill out this questionnaire to help us evaluate the effectiveness of our materials. Please be candid. Thank you.

1. Was this a home group ___ or a church-based ___ program? What church?

2. Was the study used for
   ___ a community evangelism group?
   ___ a community grow group?
   ___ a church Bible study group?

3. How would you rate the materials?

Study Guide
___ excellent ___ very good ___ good ___ fair ___ poor

Leader's Guide
___ excellent ___ very good ___ good ___ fair ___ poor

4. What were the strengths?

5. What were the weaknesses?

6. What would you suggest to improve the material?

7. In general, what was the experience of your group?

Your name (optional) ______________________________

Address ______________________________

____

8. Other comments:

(Please fold, tape, stamp, and mail. Thank you.)

CRC Publications
2850 Kalamazoo Ave. SE
Grand Rapids, MI 49560-0300